FUELING
Your Best

The 90-Day
Challenge

PAGE PUBLISHING
Conneaut Lake, PA

First originally published by Page Publishing 2023

Information contained within this publication
is for educational and entertainment purposes
and is not intended to be a substitute for a
consultation with trained professionals or health
care providers. Before starting any exercise or
health-related program, consult a physician.

Every reasonable attempt was made to give credit and
identify authors of quotes or other content provided
in this publication. Errors or omissions will be
corrected in subsequent editions. All research cited is
derived from credible institutions and publications.

Created, designed, and published by FUEL Cycle
Fitness + Something Creative, Pennsylvania USA.

ISBN 978-1-6624-7730-0 (pbk)
ISBN 978-1-6624-7732-4 (digital)

Printed in the United States of America

Challenges are what
make life interesting;
Overcoming them is what
makes life meaningful.
　　　　—Joshua J. Marine

This book belongs to:

_____

_____

_____

Ponder this...
What do you want to accomplish in the next 90 days?
Why are you taking on this challenge?

My goal for using this book is:

_____

_____

_____

I will finish the challenge by: _____(date)

FOREWORD

At the ripe old age of nine, I remember standing in my parents' bedroom looking into the mirror. I slowly turned myself sideways so I could get a side view look at my body. My patterned tights were pulled up high, and the waistband was right above my belly button. I remember lifting my cable knit sweater above my pants and staring into the mirror. My eyes were looking intently at my reflection. And more specifically, I was analyzing my bump—or what I silently referred to as my "pot belly." I pushed my stomach out as far as I could and then, sucked it back in. Then, I slowly let it stretch back out to its most natural shape.

I turned to face the other direction and took another deep breath. I was intrigued by how my belly changed shape with my breath. I noticed how I could manipulate my profile through poses and angles. But then, I would go back to letting my belly expand and see how uncomfortable I felt in my own skin. I stared at my natural belly bump with utter disgust and then sadness. I liked me, but I didn't like her—the girl I saw in the mirror whose body looked nothing like the images in the magazines and the Barbie dolls in my collection.

As my mom walked in, I quickly dropped my heavy cable knit sweater back down so she wouldn't catch me examining my body and its reflection. My sweater swung around my waist and settled just below my hips. I kept my gaze in the mirror and saw the transformation as I hid my belly under my top. I thought, *Well, at least I can cover this up.*

That is my earliest memory of judging and trying to manipulate my body. It's a memory I can recall so vividly because, for whatever reason, I thought my body needed to change and to look different to match an image I had in my mind. I saw flat bellies on other girls and in photos of celebrities who I—and others—thought were beautiful. I so badly wanted my physical appearance to fit that image of beauty and perfection that I had in my head.

Through the years, this process and these thoughts didn't change very much. I was teased for having a flat chest, and I remember searching for bras and shirts that would mask those "imperfections" as I tried to hide my insecurities. I was told that my body resembled that of a boy. I was told I had thunder thighs instead of being praised for having strong legs that could score a homerun in kickball. And in college, I overheard a frat boy telling a friend how I used to look great but not anymore with my recent weight gain.

Every insult and negative comment was like a stab that pierced my skin and left me scarred. Over the years, those stabs and scars kept coming. And what was, at first, skin deep, penetrated into my mind and soul, leaving me feeling like I would never be beautiful or skinny enough. That my flaws and the parts of my body that didn't meet society's ideals would hold me back from being liked, accepted, and appreciated.

In elementary school, I hid from the comments. I wore baggy clothes and assumed that if no one could see my body, then they wouldn't make comments. I had a gym teacher who heard the comments and saw how the boys teased me and encouraged me to play soccer (something that would ultimately change my life, leaps and bounds, and give me lifelong friendships and help me find a love for fitness).

In high school, I hid until someone noticed me, and then, I tried showing off certain parts of my body that I thought others would like. I watched my mom go through weight loss surgery and saw her confidence and relationships transform, just as her body was taking on a new shape.

In college, I went back to wearing baggy clothes, binge drank, and purged before and after Thanksgiving when I knew I would see my high school friends as I struggled with my body changing due to new habits and an out-of-control lifestyle. The only thing that kept me from spiraling out of control was my love of soccer.

Then, in grad school, I found a friend who had the same concerns about her body. She openly talked to me about her body image issues and struggles to feel comfortable in her own skin. We bonded over fitness and started running together and working out. We shared our unhealthy habits with each other but only to transform them into new habits and support healthier changes. And as we did things together that were healthy, our friends would congratulate us on our fitness and sometimes, even join us in the fitness center.

In grad school, my mentor was an avid runner and biker. He was, at least, twenty-five years my senior and his energy and attitude were infectious. I wanted to be like him when I got older. I wanted to have energy and bike to the shore and raise money for great causes.

At the same time, my dad suffered a heart attack. I remember sitting in the hospital waiting room, hoping and praying that my dad would be okay. I was determined to help and inspire him to live a healthier life. So after his recovery and when he was cleared to exercise, I made a deal with him—if my dad woke me up in the morning, I would join him at the gym, and we would workout together.

Every morning, my dad would get up at five o'clock, wake me up, and I would drag myself to the car. Sometimes, I slept during the ten-minute ride to the gym, and other times, I would speak about ten words. But we would work out and then enjoy a nice chat on the ride home. It was during those mornings that I began realizing how much I could enjoy fitness. It was also when I got into indoor cycling (because let's be honest…the only type of exercise that seems appealing whatsoever at 5:00 a.m. is the kind that involves sitting on your butt in a dark room, listening to great music, and not having to carry your own bodyweight). I was hooked and eventually, became a certified cycle instructor.

But after grad school, I hit a rough patch. In my early-to-mid-twenties, I found myself unemployed, struggling with an undiagnosed stomach disease, and feeling like I was a big failure and a complete waste of money. I felt unworthy, ugly, and unemployable. I was living on the third floor of a tiny apartment, paying $300 a month, which at times, I couldn't afford. I slept on a mattress on the floor, watched a TV I bought on a maxed-out credit card, and stored my clothes in plastic bins piled to the less than six-foot ceiling.

So why do I share this? Because the woman I am today must pay her respects to the woman I was through every phase of my life. While I struggled—physically and mentally—with my true identity and worth, I eventually found myself. Throughout the journey, I was loved and supported by my family and friends. I was loved, and I loved others with everything I had, sometimes to a fault. But I never would have landed where I am today without traveling that rough, rocky path that brought me to the happiest times in my life and into my purpose.

In 2012, I married the man of my dreams. He is the most amazing human and loved me at my best and at my worst, even when I felt far from loveable. He accepted me for who I was, knowing that I was far from perfect. He agreed to see me through my rough days and celebrate my best days, and he made me feel beautiful.

In 2015, we birthed two babies—our human son and our business baby. Our son was born in March. The moment he was born, he showed me how powerful my body was in ways I could never imagine. I mean, my body created a human. And not just any human, he was the most beautiful human I ever laid eyes on. My heart exploded, and my purpose began to bubble to the surface.

In August of the same year, my husband and I walked along the beach with my son strapped to my chest in my Ergo. We discussed our brewing plans to open a fitness studio. We already saw a space and were ready to sign the lease. We talked about the type of environment we wanted to create—a welcoming place that was nonjudgmental and was focused on a non-intimidating workout. We wanted to offer a place where couples could work out together and enjoy being fit. We wanted to eventually invite families to a place where there was something for everyone. And I wanted to bring my love of cycling and riding an indoor cycle bike to amazing playlists to people who shared my passion and those who never knew they would love sharing my passion.

And two months later, in October of 2015, our business baby was born.

Through the next four and a half years, I would be challenged, rewarded, and stretched in ways that were unimaginable to me. The business side put us through the ringer. But the purpose side, it made every tear and sleepless night worth it. My husband and I were inspiring people to lead healthier and happier lives. We were working with individuals, families, groups, and the community to provide a safe space to sweat. We brought people joy and built a community of some of the most incredible people I ever met. We were the catalyst to creating friendships and building healthy habits for those who were struggling. And when the pandemic hit, we kept a community together that learned to lean on each other when each of us felt like we might have fallen down.

We gave others—and ourselves—a reason to get up in the morning. We brought smiles when people achieved something they never thought was possible.

We encouraged others to try new things and push past their limits. And even if the financial gains were far from reality, the soul fulfilling gains kept us going.

In tandem with the founding of our fitness studio and our programs, I had the privilege of redefining what a fitness instructor should look like and how women should celebrate their bodies and not punish them. I taught young women and girls that our bodies are so much more than their physical appearance. I learned how to love myself and taught others to do the same.

And that is how and why this workbook was created. It was my way to encourage others to take small steps to help them feel better. It was about reframing, breaking ideals, and tackling taboo topics that most were never given the opportunity to discuss. I provided resources, experts, and other inspirational women to share their stories and knowledge to uplift and support others so together, we could be our best selves.

That is what I wish for you—to be inspired to become your best. I want you to reach your potential, unlock the life you always wanted to live, and challenge yourself to do things you never thought you could. And this is your chance to make it happen.

JEN CROMPTON

And suddenly you know: It's
time to start something new and
trust the magic of beginnings.
—Meister Eckhart

Intro

— — — — — — — — — — —

I created this workbook to motivate and inspire anyone with the aspiration to be challenged and grow. It was written to encourage personal fulfillment, individual success, and to help others become healthier and happier.

This workbook is dedicated to you. It's dedicated to those who want a challenge and want to make changes for the better. This workbook is geared toward giving you a chance to explore the depths of your being and to unlock your potential and help you realize all you have to offer this world.

Be challenged for the next ninety days to do things with intention and without question. Appreciate your ability to try new things, refine your strengths, and give freely to others.

Let's get started and take this journey to *FUEL your best together.*

Our FUELosophy

FUELing your best is the idea of feeling fit in all aspects of your life—from your mind to your body, to your soul…and into your pocket. You can only *be* your best when you *feel* your best. And you feel your best when you are in control and able to work toward "success" (whatever version of that definition resonates with you) in all aspects of your life.

Know that success is subjective. Your success is yours—it's what will make you fulfilled and happy. Success is not defined by the amount of money or material things you possess. Instead, it is defined by how complete you feel and happy you are with yourself.

Our *FUELosophy* is living life feeling confident in who you are and who you strive to become. You shouldn't work hard to be someone you are not. Instead, strive to become the best version of yourself and work toward your own vision of success.

The FUEL Your Best 90-Day Challenge was created to…

- Help you reach personal success through a customized, fun, and challenging process.
- Allow and invite you to be challenged differently and in a way, outside the norm.
- Inspire you to become your best version and know that incremental changes can create big changes.
- Help you understand that we must continually challenge ourselves to learn about who we are and what we can achieve to unlock our potential.
- Provide a challenge focused on being a better person and achieving your goals—not focusing on quantitative, meaningless metrics.
- Allow everyone to individually design their own path to success—because a one-size-fits-all approach is rarely practical.
- Invite you to have fun and enjoy living and learning so you can grow.

How it works

The book is separated into six sections: five categories of the challenge *ACTS* and the corresponding reflections.

The ACTS—what you need to do

The goal is to complete one *ACT* a day during the ninety-day challenge period. You can choose an *ACT* from any category and complete them in any order.

Reflection—what you need to think about

Complete a weekly reflection during each of the twelve weeks of the challenge.

Since there are seventy-five *ACTS* (with a few bonus *ACTS* in the Live and Give sections) and ninety days to complete the challenge, you can essentially take one day off each week and use that day to reflect or prepare for the week ahead.

Final ACT and reflection—what you do at the end

At the end of the challenge, there is a *final ACT*, which includes a practice in gratitude and meditation and a *final reflection.* Completing the final steps will help you identify your accomplishments and decide how to move forward while keeping your learning close.

By the end of the ninety days, all the *ACTS* and *reflections* should be completed, and you can feel confident in your progress toward obtaining a deeper understanding of who you are and your potential to reach personal success and fulfillment.

Let's Get Started

First, set your start and end dates and commit to completing what you can in the next ninety days. Remember, there are seventy-five *ACTS* and twelve reflections to complete within the ninety days. Read through some of the *ACTS* in each category and get a sense of what you will need to do daily. Once you have a solid idea of what you want to accomplish, set your overarching goal and map out what it will take to get you there.

Each Day

For the ninety days of the challenge, each day, open this workbook and select an *ACT* (or reflection once a week). Complete the *ACT*. Then, fill out the quick *ACT* reflection.

Each Week

Each week, fill out your weekly reflection (which is different from the daily *ACT* reflection) and make sure you made progress completing your daily *ACTS*.

On Day 90

On day ninety, complete your final *ACT* and reflection. Set aside a few minutes to thank yourself for what you accomplished. Be proud and be confident. Review what you wrote and take time to appreciate what you invested in self-improvement.

Ongoing

We offer an FYB (FUEL Your Best) online community to help you complete the *ACTS* and offer support whenever you need it. You aren't required to participate, but you are more than welcome to get involved. Visit fybfit.com/workbook to join the community and help you stay motivated and reach your goals.

And that's it! It is simple, effective, and it can be life-changing if you put in the effort.

So let's get started…

LIVE

- - - - - - - - - - - -

Be fearless in the pursuit of what sets your soul on fire.

Live ACTS

Ponder this…

How are you living your life?

What are you doing with your days, weeks, months, and years?

What feels good? What doesn't?

What would you like to change?

Live ACTS focus on how we operate day-to-day and what we do to make the most of our precious time on this planet. We must put our oxygen mask on first, so you have to evaluate how you live and make incremental changes to ensure you are living your best life in a way that makes sense and fulfills you.

Once you can do that for yourself, you can focus on others and give the world what you know you have to offer.

You have one shot at *life*. So why not give it your best shot?

Complete these fifteen *live ACTS* plus learn more about how you live now, how you want to live, and what will fulfill and push you to live on purpose.

1. Go on a digital detox.

While technology can do wonderful things for us, it can also cause negative effects if we let it. Therefore, it is always a good idea to take a break and get back to "real life" without the distraction of the digital world.

For this *ACT*, avoid using technology for a full twenty-four hours. That means no phone, no computer, and no other way to access email, texts, calls, or social media. Give up watching TV and anything related to technology. Challenge yourself to figure out other ways to connect, learn, and be entertained.

Reflection

_____

_____

_____

_____

_____

_____

_____

_____

_____

_____

_____

_____

_____

_____

_____

_____

_____

_____

_____

_____

_____

_____

_____

2. Be mindful.

Being mindful means being present in the moment without thinking about the past, future, or anything outside of what is happening *right now.*

For an entire day, be mindful. Take note of your actions and your words. Be present and at the moment. Observe what you're doing as if you were a spectator of your own life. Think about your actions and the why behind them. Consider how you feel. Observe your interactions with others, your inner dialogue and self-talk, and how your mood and energy move throughout the day. (For tips and tools for meditating, see the resources section.)

Reflection

_____
_____
_____
_____
_____
_____
_____
_____
_____
_____
_____
_____
_____
_____
_____
_____
_____
_____
_____
_____
_____
_____
_____

3. Meditate.

Meditation is a practice that uses a technique—such as mindfulness or focusing the mind on a particular object, thought, or activity—to train attention and awareness. The goal is to achieve a clear and emotionally calm mental state. There are various meditation techniques (and what works for one person may or may not work for the next), so most people try more than one to find what truly works for their lifestyle and mental state.

Take one to five minutes of your day to meditate. This meditation can take any form you would like—whichever meditation you feel will be beneficial. This could mean taking five long, deep breaths or sitting in silence, focusing on your breath for the full five minutes. If you attempt one type of meditation and it doesn't work, try another. (For tips and tools for meditating, see the resources section.)

Reflection

_____
_____
_____
_____
_____
_____
_____
_____
_____
_____
_____
_____
_____
_____
_____
_____
_____
_____
_____
_____
_____

4. Listen.

We have two ears and one mouth, so we can listen twice as much as we speak. However, most of us talk a lot, and if we aren't the ones speaking during a conversation, we may be thinking about the next thing we need to say. So let's be more conscious of this action and learn to listen.

This ACT is to take time during your day and truly engage in the ACT of listening. Choose a person or conversation and commit to being fully present and listening.

Throughout the day, be an active listener by focusing on the words spoken. Avoid thinking about the next thing you want to say or want to discuss. Be a true passenger in the conversation and focus on the words shared with you.

Reflection

_____
_____
_____
_____
_____
_____
_____
_____
_____
_____
_____
_____
_____
_____
_____
_____
_____
_____
_____
_____
_____
_____
_____

5. Make "me" time.

Self-care is not selfish in a negative way—it is necessary. We all need time to ourselves. We need to unwind, replenish, and do the work to energize our minds and bodies.

So plan a day for you. It's "me time"—an entire day dedicated to doing whatever it is that you want to do and not doing things that you think others need you to do. If taking a full day to focus on yourself seems overwhelming, try a half-day or a block of time, that is at least four hours. Make yourself the priority and ask yourself what you really want to do with that time. *Pro Tip:* Planning for this ACT is very effective.

Reflection

_____
_____
_____
_____
_____
_____
_____
_____
_____
_____
_____
_____
_____
_____
_____
_____
_____
_____
_____
_____
_____
_____
_____

6. Enjoy a FNO.

"All work and no play make Jack a dull boy. It also contributes heavily to your daily stress." So let's avoid focusing too heavily on one and not the other and work to find that balance. After all, a day or evening of laughter with the right person (or group) can be the best and most effective stress reliever.

Grab a friend or a group and enjoy a Fun Night Out! This can be anything from going to a comedy show to watching your favorite band or merely enjoying dinner and drinks. Make it an evening to relax, unwind, and have a good time.

Reflection

_____
_____
_____
_____
_____
_____
_____
_____
_____
_____
_____
_____
_____
_____
_____
_____
_____
_____
_____
_____
_____
_____
_____

7. Plan a "cation."

When we work in the corporate world, we often get vacation days. Unfortunately, too often, we consider these days sacred or feel guilty using them. Vacation days were created for a reason—we all need time to unwind and get out of work mode.

So whether or not traveling is a good or feasible idea, you need a "cation." So plan any type of "cation" that works for you and requires you to unplug, get out of work mode and into vacation mode, and invite you to live and laugh. Plan and take a vacation to a location you have on your bucket list. Or consider a staycation and stay home and veg out. Or you can even plan a *lo*-cation, where you explore the city or place you are in as if you were a tourist.

Reflection

_____
_____
_____
_____
_____
_____
_____
_____
_____
_____
_____
_____
_____
_____
_____
_____
_____
_____
_____
_____
_____
_____

8. Write a letter.

Some are great at expressing their emotions in words, and others are best on paper. The advantage of writing your emotions down is that it allows for an uninterrupted flow and then, time to reflect before actually sharing those words with someone else.

Grab a pen, paper, envelope, and a stamp, and write an old-fashioned letter. Consider writing a letter to a loved one, a friend, or even an anonymous letter to a person or child who needs a "pick-me-up." Get writing and make sure you send the letter.

Reflection

_____

_____

_____

_____

_____

_____

_____

_____

_____

_____

_____

_____

_____

_____

_____

_____

_____

_____

_____

_____

9. Make a phone call.

Remember when you used to have to call someone to have a conversation? Now, the convenience of texting requires much less work to reach out and "talk" to someone. However, we all know that the nuances in tone and intention are hard to emit via text even while using emojis. So let's bring back the art of the good, old-fashioned phone call.

Pick up your phone and call someone. Consider calling someone you haven't spoken to in a while or someone you meant to call but didn't. If the person you called doesn't answer, leave a message or call again until you get to have that conversation. Be prepared for an unscripted phone conversation and take your time chatting. Enjoy the spontaneity of the topics and see where it takes you.

Reflection

_____
_____
_____
_____
_____
_____
_____
_____
_____
_____
_____
_____
_____
_____
_____
_____
_____
_____
_____
_____
_____

10. Take action.

We all put things off. Big or small, we tend to procrastinate and keep certain actions on our to-do list with the intention of moving it to the completed list. However, some actions have a roadblock or challenge that prevents us from achieving them.

Think about something that you want to do but keep putting it off for one reason or another. It could be something simple such as filing papers or organizing your home office. Or it could be something more significant like paying an overdue bill or sending a meaningful thank you note. Whatever it is—big or small—remove the option of not doing it and commit to taking action to get it done.

Reflection

_____
_____
_____
_____
_____
_____
_____
_____
_____
_____
_____
_____
_____
_____
_____
_____
_____
_____
_____
_____
_____
_____

11. Do something that scares you.

Doing something that scares you requires you to muster the strength and confidence that you didn't think you had. It forces you to feel emotions that are out of the norm and then navigate your way through to the other side. When you get to the other side, you are a changed person.

Find something that scares you. Conquer a challenge, engage in a conversation, or put yourself in a situation that you would otherwise avoid. If you feel the butterflies, you know that you faced your "fear" and are growing and changing.

Reflection

_____
_____
_____
_____
_____
_____
_____
_____
_____
_____
_____
_____
_____
_____
_____
_____
_____
_____
_____
_____
_____
_____

12. Get uncomfortable.

Have you ever heard the quote, "get comfortable with feeling uncomfortable?" Doing something that makes you feel a little uncomfortable forces you to grow. When we get uncomfortable, we are traveling out of our comfort zone, and it is then we can start to discover parts of our hidden selves and find talents, or passions, we never knew we had.

Find something out of your comfort zone and go for it. Forget about what could go wrong or how you may feel. Growth and excitement are found just on the other side of comfort. If you never get out of your comfort zone, you'll never reach your potential.

Reflection

_____
_____
_____
_____
_____
_____
_____
_____
_____
_____
_____
_____
_____
_____
_____
_____
_____
_____
_____
_____
_____
_____
_____
_____
_____

13. Challenge yourself.

When you challenge yourself, you change yourself. Every challenge you face and overcome and every challenge that buries you provides a lesson. From that lesson, you can further distill who you are and further define your goals. Pick a challenge and give it a shot. If you succeed, you win. If you don't succeed and you learn, you still win.

Challenge yourself to do something that feels just beyond your reach. Identify a goal or situation that you aspire to conquer. Maybe you want to start a business or launch a product. Or maybe you want to run a mile or finish a race. Whatever the challenge is, face it.

Reflection

_____
_____
_____
_____
_____
_____
_____
_____
_____
_____
_____
_____
_____
_____
_____
_____
_____
_____
_____
_____

14. Make a list.

Lists are a helpful way to organize your thoughts or actions. They provide a framework and help prioritize or make sense of a set of information. The bonus of list-making is that it can help you visualize and solidify a set of ideas or goals. In other words, creating a bucket list gives you something to aim for—and putting it on paper makes it seem more realistic and makes you more accountable.

Make a list of any kind. Make a bucket list, a to-do list, or places-to-visit list. Don't edit or cross things off—just go ahead and make a list. Then, once complete, take some time to review the info or any revisions you want to make. After your list is complete, tie an action to it. This can be a deadline to finish the list, a time to revisit the list, and etc.

Reflection

_____
_____
_____
_____
_____
_____
_____
_____
_____
_____
_____
_____
_____
_____
_____
_____
_____
_____
_____
_____
_____

15. Create a vision board.

A vision board is a visual representation of your future and everything it holds. Maybe you want to hit an income benchmark, start a family, or travel to new places. Your vision board should hold both personal and professional visions for your future.

Make a vision board that can be placed somewhere in plain sight where you will be forced to see it every day. To create the board, use print-outs, magazines, or anything you want and create a board you can look at often. Use pieces that inspire you to think big, reach your goals, and live the life you dream. By seeing your vision, you will be reminded of where you want to go, and each day, you will get a little closer to turning that vision into a reality.

Reflection

_____

_____

_____

_____

_____

_____

_____

_____

_____

_____

_____

_____

_____

_____

_____

_____

_____

_____

_____

_____

_____

16. Create a personal mantra.

Who are you? What do you stand for? What words do you live by? A personal mantra is a guiding statement of what you believe in and what drives your decisions. It will remind you of who you are and what you believe in and how to be true to yourself. *If you stand for nothing, you'll fall for anything.* That quote has been attributed to so many different people, and rather than figuring out who said it first, just say it to yourself. Refine what it is that you stand for...and make it your mantra. Your mantra can be simple or more detailed. Write it, rewrite it. Once you feel good about it, use it to drive your life decisions, mindset, and overall mood. Your mantra is fluid and can (and most likely will) change as you transform. However, your mantra should always bring you back to who you are at the core and remind you how you want to live your life.

Reflection

_____

_____

_____

_____

_____

_____

_____

_____

_____

_____

_____

_____

_____

_____

_____

_____

_____

_____

_____

_____

17. Be positive for an entire day.

A smile is contagious. A good attitude creates a frequency that transmits enough to light an entire room. A simple switch from a negative outlook to a positive one can change the trajectory of your whole day. Recalling our day offers a subjective interpretation of our true actions. However, as we become more mindful, we may find out that we are more negative than we initially let on.

In our lives, we attract what we offer. So positive actions bring positivity. So be mindful, and practice being positive for an entire day by thinking positive thoughts, saying positive words, and doing positive things. When you feel negativity creeping in, kick it to the curb and replace it with something positive.

Reflection

_____
_____
_____
_____
_____
_____
_____
_____
_____
_____
_____
_____
_____
_____
_____
_____
_____
_____
_____
_____
_____
_____
_____
_____

18. Talk to a stranger.

You never know who the person is next to you until you strike up a conversation. And you never know what you can learn until you listen.

Please do not put yourself in danger, but consider striking up a conversation with someone you don't know. Maybe it is at the grocery store, local coffee shop, or at the gym. You can even consider chatting with someone you may kind of know but don't really know as well as you'd like. Take the time to talk to a stranger and learn something new. You will likely be surprised by what you learn about the other person—and it may even create a shift in perspective.

Reflection

_____

_____

_____

_____

_____

_____

_____

_____

_____

_____

_____

_____

_____

_____

_____

_____

_____

_____

_____

_____

19. Plant a seed.

Contrary to the concept of overnight success, ideas, plans, and incredible actions, it does not happen overnight. Behind those successes is a trail made of hard work, dedication, and carefully planted seeds that have had a chance to flourish and bloom.

Put some thought into what you want to see grow and flourish in your life. Then, take the time to plant a seed—the beginnings and foundation of what you want in the future. This is a symbolic seed. A seed is an idea, thought, or intention you are ready to bring to fruition. In time, it will eventually grow into something bigger if you water it enough. Because big things grow after they are planted and nurtured.

Plant the seed now and enjoy the fruits of your labor when it blooms. And remember, growth and transforming into true beauty may take time, so practice being patient.

Reflection

_____
_____
_____
_____
_____
_____
_____
_____
_____
_____
_____
_____
_____
_____
_____
_____
_____
_____
_____
_____
_____
_____

20. *Pause before you respond.*

An essential mantra to remember is that *there is power in the pause.*

We often respond to others and situations without too much thought—we simply react. Instead of reacting to something that may evoke an emotion (maybe a text message that gets your heart pumping or a conversation that feels uncomfortable), take a moment and pause. Use the power of the pause to consider the true context of the situation and the actual meaning of what someone said or did. Then, determine the best way to respond based on what *really* happened and how you want to get to the next step or find a resolution. There is power in the pause that can make your reactive actions more meaningful and productive.

Reflection

_____

_____

_____

_____

_____

_____

_____

_____

_____

_____

_____

_____

_____

_____

_____

_____

_____

_____

_____

_____

_____

_____

21. Evaluate your "company."

We are viewed by the company we keep. Our general thoughts, actions, and attitudes are influenced by those around us. Therefore, if we want to feel or perform a certain way, we should surround ourselves with those who make us feel and ACT like our best. However, we also want to make sure that we are not living in an echo chamber and can use our company as a sounding board to keep us on track.

Take time to evaluate your company. With whom do you spend the majority of your time? Are those people the ones you want to be around and be like? If so, find out why you enjoy their company and what you appreciate about each person. If you do not feel confident about the company you keep, consider making a change. Remember, where and how you spend your time is your choice.

Reflection

_____
_____
_____
_____
_____
_____
_____
_____
_____
_____
_____
_____
_____
_____
_____
_____
_____
_____
_____
_____
_____
_____

GIVE

- - - - - - - - - - -

> We make a living by what
> we get, but we make a
> life by what we give.
> —Winston Churchill

Give ACTS

Ponder this...

What do you give to others?

What *can* you give to others?

What do you care about?

What purpose do you feel is important?

What cause do you feel is much greater than yourself?

Do you give your time or resources to anyone or any organization? How does that make you feel?

We get most of our satisfaction in life, not by what we get but by what we give. Giving our time, our attention, and our resources to others is how we grow as individuals. We often feel fulfilled when we can share our talents with others, help those we care about reach their potential, and when we support others on the journey to their dreams.

While we must take care of ourselves before we are able to really give to others, that does not mean that you must wait until you reach your potential to focus on the art of giving. Remember that, sometimes, even the simplest "giving ACTS" can yield amazing results for both the giver and the receiver.

Complete these fifteen *give ACTS* and learn how and what you can give to others, then reflect on how it makes you feel.

1. Pay it forward.

One November, I got word that I secured my biggest client contract for the following year. I remember it vividly because it was one of a handful of emails that have professionally given me space to breathe and feel "okay." I felt that wave of emotion sitting inside a Starbucks. I worked my tail off to keep the contract and was so relieved when I got the final green light and thought about the impact a single conversation, email, phone call, or ACT of kindness could have on a person. As a way to thank the universe for my exciting news, I bought a $50 gift card at Starbucks, handed it to the cashier, and asked them to use it for the next few orders until the balance was depleted. I sat silently and watched as customers were told to put their wallets away because this one was "on us."

Think back. Were you one of those customers? Did someone unexpectedly do something amazing for you? The universe uses others to show its support for you. So it's your time to pay it forward and do something kind.

Pro Tip: If this hasn't happened to you in a while, start the process. Pay for the drink of the person behind you. Watch that ripple of kindness turn into a wave.

Reflection

_____

_____

_____

_____

_____

_____

_____

_____

_____

_____

_____

_____

_____

_____

_____

_____

_____

2. Make a meaningful gift.

When you get to a point in your life where you have what you want, you may realize how physical things really don't serve you. While purchasing a nice luxury item for a friend or family member is a nice thing to do and he/she may appreciate it, sometimes, the meaning of that expensive item is translated into trying to "buy" one's affection. It can also be perceived as a substitute for other absent emotions.

For the next holiday, birthday, or just for fun, make something meaningful to give to a friend or loved one. Making something can be as simple as a handwritten card, a personalized piece of art, a playlist, or a photo in a frame. Whatever you make, remember that it doesn't have to be perfect. It is less about the object and much more about the meaning and the effort behind it. (*Bonus:* Enjoy their reaction.)

Reflection

_____
_____
_____
_____
_____
_____
_____
_____
_____
_____
_____
_____
_____
_____
_____
_____
_____
_____
_____
_____
_____
_____

3. Donate your time.

While monetary donations to people and causes can make a huge difference, sometimes they are not possible. And sometimes, no matter how much money is given to a cause, it will still need humans to do the work.

Pick an organization or cause that you feel connected to and spend some time making a difference. This can mean doing some hands-on work volunteering or using your skills to offer a service the organization may need. If you don't have a specific organization or cause you want to support, start researching and find one that aligns with your core values and personal mission.

Reflection

_____
_____
_____
_____
_____
_____
_____
_____
_____
_____
_____
_____
_____
_____
_____
_____
_____
_____
_____
_____
_____

4. Give someone your time.

Time is our most precious finite resource. We cannot alter the amount of time we have in this life. However, what is up to us is how we choose to spend that time. Meaning, there are always twenty-four hours in a day and sixty minutes in an hour. And how many of those hours and days we get to experience in our lifetime is not up to us. However, what is up to us is how we choose to spend those hours and minutes.

What we do with our days is what shapes our lives. Too often, we don't use our time as wisely as we should, and in hindsight, we may end up regretting those decisions. So rather than allowing it to waste away, use some of your precious time by giving it away to someone else. Giving your time can be as simple as going to a friend's house to chat and offering uninterrupted time spent together. Or maybe it is lending an ear through the phone and mindfully listening to the voice on the other end. Your time is precious, and therefore, it is the most intimate and kind gift you can offer.

Reflection

_____
_____
_____
_____
_____
_____
_____
_____
_____
_____
_____
_____
_____
_____
_____
_____
_____
_____
_____
_____
_____
_____

5. Listen.

Listening is not easy. Our brains are consumed with millions of thoughts throughout the day, and they become a distraction when we attempt to focus on what others want to share. But listening is a skill that can be learned. And to be good at it, it is one that must be practiced.

Without hesitation, distractions, or focusing on your responses—take the time to truly listen to someone else during a conversation, speech, or in another situation. Listen intently and allow yourself to become truly absorbed at the moment and really focus on the words that are spoken and the emotions they evoke. Avoid thinking about what is behind or ahead of you, and refrain from expressing knee-jerk reactions and responses. Allow yourself to just listen and "be."

Reflection

_____
_____
_____
_____
_____
_____
_____
_____
_____
_____
_____
_____
_____
_____
_____
_____
_____
_____
_____
_____

6. Give away your "stuff."

Our stuff is often a collection of things that we use to create an outward representation of who we are or who we want to be. While we often use these external objects or things to create a situation or image that we think meets others or our own expectations, we often don't need those things and may even be using them to hide our true identities.

Take a look at your "stuff." Create an inventory of what you actually use (not "plan to use someday") and what you don't use. What do you love? What do you need? What can you give away and share with someone else who would appreciate it more than you? Find the stuff you don't use or need, donate it, gift it to someone in need, or give it away freely, knowing that someone else will appreciate it.

Reflection

_____

_____

_____

_____

_____

_____

_____

_____

_____

_____

_____

_____

_____

_____

_____

_____

_____

_____

_____

_____

_____

_____

7. Give your knowledge.

We are all experts in something. We may use our expertise for our professions or side hustles or win the first-place trophy at Quizzo. Our knowledge is built from our experiences and what you know now took your lifetime to learn. Part of your responsibility and gift is to share that knowledge with others.

Regardless of what it is that you know, take time to share it with someone who could benefit. Share your thoughts, knowledge, and/or ideas that are swirling around in your brain. Share fun facts, lessons learned, or any information you feel is valuable, and the recipient will appreciate it.

Reflection

_____

_____

_____

_____

_____

_____

_____

_____

_____

_____

_____

_____

_____

_____

_____

_____

_____

_____

_____

_____

_____

8. Lend a helping hand.

Help is often difficult to request. Whether it's because you don't want to put a burden on someone else or you have a layer of shame or embarrassment that you need outside assistance—help is needed more often than many would imagine.

Take a moment to think about those around you who may need help in one way or another. Maybe it's an odd job, moving furniture, writing letters, organizing, or something else. Has someone recently directly or indirectly asked for help? Do you know someone who could use help but will likely never ask? Whatever the situation, reach out and offer to lend a hand and insist that your offer be considered. Big or small, offering a helping hand can make a big difference.

Reflection

_____
_____
_____
_____
_____
_____
_____
_____
_____
_____
_____
_____
_____
_____
_____
_____
_____
_____
_____
_____
_____

9. Ask about their day (and care about the response).

Too often, we get into our own routines. We check our to-dos off our list, and we are consumed by making sure we are prepared and able to complete what is coming next. But how often are we truly focusing on the well-being of someone else? Do you really know how your partner's, kid's, or best friend's day was today?

Go out of your way to ask someone—anyone that matters to you—about his/her day. Ask about what went right that day. Then, take the time to truly, actively listen to the response. Ask relevant follow-up questions and resist the urge to insert your own stories unless you are specifically asked to share. Absorb their comments and appreciate what they share.

Reflection

_____
_____
_____
_____
_____
_____
_____
_____
_____
_____
_____
_____
_____
_____
_____
_____
_____
_____
_____
_____

10. Give credit.

Ever get an unexpected shout of recognition that made you feel good about yourself? Maybe you killed it in your last presentation, contributed to a project that went exceptionally well, or offered an idea that really worked out. When someone acknowledged your contribution and offered a compliment for your hard work, did it feel good?

Sometimes, we overlook the opportunity to give credit where credit is due. When we ignore these opportunities, the good that someone offers may feel like it goes unnoticed. So be that person for someone else. Find an opportunity—or simply don't overlook an existing one—to give a compliment or offer attribution to someone in your personal or professional life. Let someone know that what they did was noticed and appreciated. Or offer a kudos to someone who shared a great idea or did something incredible that made a positive impact on you or your environment.

Reflection

_____
_____
_____
_____
_____
_____
_____
_____
_____
_____
_____
_____
_____
_____
_____
_____
_____
_____
_____
_____
_____
_____

11. Give thanks.

We operate at our best when we are in a state of gratitude. When we can make decisions out of love and kindness, we avoid operating in a state of fear. Therefore, we can make more thoughtful decisions and lead with a clearer mind. When we are grateful and show our gratitude, we vibrate at our highest energy and lift others up to meet us. That is the place where the universe wants us to be and where we feel and can *ACT* our best.

Take time—through morning prayer, repeating a mantra, journaling, or whichever way works for you—to say thank you and give thanks to the universe that you are alive, breathing, and able to see another sunrise. Giving thanks regularly may cause an abundance of great things to happen in your life. So accept that greatness with open arms and know that you are deserving of all the good things when you are grateful for who you are and what you have.

Reflection

_____
_____
_____
_____
_____
_____
_____
_____
_____
_____
_____
_____
_____
_____
_____
_____
_____
_____
_____
_____
_____
_____

12. Share a story.

Our lives are built around stories. They excite, motivate, teach, and entertain us. We play the roles of storyteller, story listener, or are in a state of an actor of a story that has not yet been told. Whatever we go through or wherever we are, we are writing our stories and creating a journey that others can retell and appreciate. It's our job to share this story when the time is right.

Offer a story of success, hardship, or encouragement to someone who needs it. Share a story about yourself, something you saw or experienced, or a story you heard that positively impacted you. Share that story with someone else and discuss the meaning together. Take note if the story resonates differently than it did in your perspective.

Reflection

_____
_____
_____
_____
_____
_____
_____
_____
_____
_____
_____
_____
_____
_____
_____
_____
_____
_____
_____
_____

13. Give your support.

Everyone who looks like they have it held together has someone (or a team of people) who applies the glue to keep them in one piece. One of the most powerful things you can do for others is to show your support and be that glue by understanding their mission, goals, or vision.

Support can be offered by attending events, purchasing a product or service, sharing the word about a new endeavor, or simply being on the cheering squad with your voice heard loud and clear. The people whom you support will absolutely appreciate it and know you care—and that support can make a subtle but profound impact on their success. Find an opportunity to offer and give support to someone in your life that you are on his/her side, and you are rooting for success.

Reflection

_____
_____
_____
_____
_____
_____
_____
_____
_____
_____
_____
_____
_____
_____
_____
_____
_____
_____
_____
_____
_____

14. Show up.

Often, the hardest part is showing up. There are always a million reasons why you "can't" attend an event, go to a party, enjoy a night out. But while showing up may be the hardest part, it is also the most important and the part that really matters.

Achieve this *ACT* by making a mindful effort to choose a specific way to show up for a friend, a loved one, or for yourself. Note the impact that "showing up" can make and then commit to making this an ongoing effort.

Reflection

_____
_____
_____
_____
_____
_____
_____
_____
_____
_____
_____
_____
_____
_____
_____
_____
_____
_____
_____
_____
_____
_____

15. Share your talent.

What is your true talent? Are you an incredible photographer? Are you a really great storyteller? Are you a whiz at teaching others how to shoot a basketball? Your talents are your gifts, and they are meant to be shared and appreciated. When you share your talent, you are offering an opportunity for others to appreciate what you do well. And as a bonus, sometimes, sharing your talent can open doors to new opportunities that you didn't even know existed.

Find someone (or a group) who can benefit from your talent(s). Take time to share your talents for fun, or for their benefit, and enjoy offering your gifts to others.

Reflection

_____
_____
_____
_____
_____
_____
_____
_____
_____
_____
_____
_____
_____
_____
_____
_____
_____
_____
_____
_____
_____
_____
_____

16. Give someone an opportunity.

In my career, I can trace every great opportunity or "win" back to someone who was willing to give me an opportunity or "take a chance" on me and my ideas and talents. There are at least a half dozen of these mentors and aspirational leaders that I can think about, and I am immediately grateful for their support and willingness to support and elevate me to the next level.

And I am not the only one. Successful people will often attribute "wins" along their journey to others who offered a break or an opportunity. Maybe it was an opportunity to share their idea, sell their product, or show support and truly believe in a mission. While these "breaks" are a combination of being prepared and the universe offering direction, these opportunities shape lives and push others to pursue their purpose. So why not be that person? Find a way to give a deserving person an opportunity. You never know, it could change their life—and it may change yours.

Reflection

_____

_____

_____

_____

_____

_____

_____

_____

_____

_____

_____

_____

_____

_____

_____

_____

_____

_____

_____

_____

_____

_____

17. Give freely.

When people operate from a place of fear or insecurity, they often give with the intention to receive. They offer opportunities or support but with the underlying goal of getting the same or more in return. People give with expectations because they assume they "owe" someone else; therefore, it is an obligation. But there is another way to give—and that is to give freely.

When you give freely, without expectations of anything in return, you are liberated. It's an incredible feeling and allows you to offer something simply because it is what you choose to do. Give something out of the kindness of your heart and give with purpose. By removing the expectations of a return or acknowledgment, you will give with all you have and feel truly fulfilled by the action.

Reflection

_____

_____

_____

_____

_____

_____

_____

_____

_____

_____

_____

_____

_____

_____

_____

_____

_____

_____

_____

_____

_____

_____

18. Give love.

Love is love is love—and it is what makes the world go round. It is the most basic human psychological necessity and has the power to change what is bad to good and allows us to forgive what may seem unforgivable. Love has the power to turn stress and unrest to calm and security. And when we feel loved, we can give love.

The most undeniable surefire way to make the world a happier place is to give love. It is free, it is plentiful, and it is necessary. And the more love you give the world, the more it will love you back.

Reflection

_____
_____
_____
_____
_____
_____
_____
_____
_____
_____
_____
_____
_____
_____
_____
_____
_____
_____
_____
_____
_____

LAUGH

There is nothing in the world
so irresistibly contagious as
laughter and good humor.
—Charles Dickens

Laugh Acts

Ponder this…

Do you laugh every day?
What makes you laugh?
Who makes you laugh?
What do you enjoy?

Learning to laugh is absolutely one of the keys to living a healthy and happy life. Laughing is nature's medicine, and using it as a way to cope with situations and connect with others can help reduce stress and anxiety.

Laughter enters when distraction leaves. When you are entirely focused on having fun, you can let yourself laugh and enjoy life. Laughing leads to a feeling of freedom and happiness, which helps us grow.

Laugh ACTS focus on learning how to have fun and taking the time to focus on what makes you smile and makes your heart happy. It's about having a full-on belly laugh and being in the moment so you can enjoy what is happening here and now.

Complete these fifteen *laugh* ACTS and start smiling more, loving deeper, and laughing harder.

1. Tell a joke.

Jokes, no matter how silly or ridiculous, are intended to make us laugh and smile. They are little comments that can break up an intense moment, lighten the mood, and allow us to share a chuckle.

So think of (or find) a joke and tell it to someone. The joke can be simple; it can be a dad joke, a funny joke, or a super silly joke. Don't overthink it. Whatever type of joke you choose, share the joke, and share the smile. *Pro Tip:* If, at first, the joke doesn't succeed, try a different one.

Reflection

_____
_____
_____
_____
_____
_____
_____
_____
_____
_____
_____
_____
_____
_____
_____
_____
_____
_____
_____
_____
_____

2. Watch something funny.

Most of us have a go-to that we know will make us laugh. For instance, some think videos of people wiping out are hilarious (pending that the individuals aren't actually injured). Or maybe talking dogs are more your speed.

Check out a YouTube clip, Insta story, your favorite movie, or your own video that always cracks you up. Take a moment (or a few moments) to let go of any other thoughts and watch something that will make you laugh. Enjoy the humor and let that humor make you feel a little lighter.

Reflection

_____
_____
_____
_____
_____
_____
_____
_____
_____
_____
_____
_____
_____
_____
_____
_____
_____
_____
_____
_____
_____
_____

3. Get perspective.

In life, there will always be situations when we feel stressed, upset, or another combination of emotions that are outside of the feelings of contentment and happiness. These situations are inevitable, and it's more than okay to feel less than happy. However, we want to acknowledge these emotions and then, move through them and avoid letting them hold us back or make us feel debilitated.

When you find yourself in a situation where you feel less than happy, take a few moments to reframe how you perceive the situation—in other words, *get perspective.* Take a step back and evaluate the situation at hand on its own and in the context of the bigger picture. This will allow you to be more objective. When you change how you see the situation, it may help you change your thoughts. Let this change in perspective shift your thoughts and actions toward a more content and happier place rather than remaining a source of stress or discontent.

Reflection

_____
_____
_____
_____
_____
_____
_____
_____
_____
_____
_____
_____
_____
_____
_____
_____
_____
_____
_____
_____
_____

4. Read a book.

Books are an invitation to explore new topics, new worlds, and stretch your imagination. They are windows to new experiences and a way to learn or escape with your mind and without having to physically go anywhere.

A short book, a picture book, or a book that is on your reading list—whatever book it is, set aside time and commit. Keep that time commitment as your time to read and rid yourself of thoughts of guilt that make you feel like you should be doing something else. If you are having trouble dedicating a chunk of time long enough to get lost in your book of choice, consider dedicating five, ten, or fifteen minutes each day to uninterrupted reading. Start small and add time when it works. If you find you can squeeze more time into your commitment, gradually increase the time until you find a nice balance.

Reflection

_____
_____
_____
_____
_____
_____
_____
_____
_____
_____
_____
_____
_____
_____
_____
_____
_____
_____
_____
_____
_____
_____

5. Say "I love you."

Those three little words pack more of a punch than most other three-word sentences. The idea of giving your love and expressing it both in your actions and words is something we crave and help us improve our relationships and moods. We must not take the love we have, or give, for granted and instead, express it in meaningful ways.

Say "I love you" for the first time or the millionth time. Say it unconditionally. Say it often. And mean it when you say it. Life is short enough that you could never say it too much, and sometimes, we don't realize that we haven't told someone that means a lot to us that we love them in quite some time.

Reflection

_____
_____
_____
_____
_____
_____
_____
_____
_____
_____
_____
_____
_____
_____
_____
_____
_____
_____
_____
_____
_____

6. Teach a kid (or some-one else) a joke.

Jokes are fun to tell—and they are also fun to teach. Explaining why a joke is funny or sharing that double entendre that makes everyone giggle is worth the conversation.

Consider dissecting a knock-knock joke or a riddle. Tell the joke, then take the time to teach the joke to a kid—or someone else—who will laugh and appreciate learning it. Enjoy every aspect of the experience—learning the joke, telling it, and teaching it—and then, tell the other person to pass it along.

Reflection

_____
_____
_____
_____
_____
_____
_____
_____
_____
_____
_____
_____
_____
_____
_____
_____
_____
_____
_____
_____
_____
_____
_____

7. Create "art."

Art is subjective, and "the beauty is in the eye of the beholder." There is no set definition of the meaning of art. Whatever you feel is art, it becomes art. Ultimately, art is a creative outlet and gives the artist the opportunity to express a thought, story, or emotion.

Think about the type of art you want to create and get started. You can begin with a single stroke of a paintbrush, a pencil line, or kneading a brick of clay into an abstract shape. Take the time to color, paint, draw, or mold a sculpture. The beauty of art is in the eye of the beholder, and it should be meaningful to you—the creator.

Reflection

_____
_____
_____
_____
_____
_____
_____
_____
_____
_____
_____
_____
_____
_____
_____
_____
_____
_____
_____
_____
_____

8. Make someone laugh.

Laughing is contagious, and there is no better feeling than the pure joy that comes with sharing a laugh. The key is to discover what others find funny and to help bring more of that into their lives, and with that, you can share more giggles, joy, and the warmth of many smiles.

Do something funny. Or choose something funny to watch, or share, and make someone else laugh. If you are with the person, take a look at their face—their mouth and eyes—and watch how they change when they laugh. Revel in sharing the emotion.

Reflection

_____
_____
_____
_____
_____
_____
_____
_____
_____
_____
_____
_____
_____
_____
_____
_____
_____
_____
_____
_____
_____
_____

9. Dance in your car.

Dance like no one is watching—even if someone *is* watching. The sound of music and the movement of our bodies is something that can immediately lift our spirits and easily change our mood for the better. So when we feel a little less than our best, one way to slip into a renewed mindset is to let loose and shake our tail feathers.

For this *ACT*, when stopped in your driveway or at a red light (safely), put on a song that you love and bust out your best car dancing moves. Just let go of your inhibitions and dance by yourself or with a passenger and ignore any confused expressions from onlookers. But of course, do this safely and ensure you never take your hands off the wheel of a moving vehicle or lose control while your car is in drive.

Reflection

_____
_____
_____
_____
_____
_____
_____
_____
_____
_____
_____
_____
_____
_____
_____
_____
_____
_____
_____
_____
_____
_____

10. Write a letter to your future self.

It's in our nature to think about the future and to imagine where we will be, who we will be, and the life we will be living as we evolve and grow. Without imagining the future and daydreaming about our accomplishments, we will be void of a sense of purpose and unable to refine our vision and live our mission.

Think about who you want to be in five or ten years. Where do you want to be mentally, physically, and financially? Choose your timeframe—five or ten years—and take a few minutes to write a letter to your vision of your future self. Tell your future self who you are today, what you want for your future, and what you hope you will have accomplished by that point. Place your letter in an envelope and seal it. Stash the letter in a safe hiding spot and keep it until you hit that future date.

Reflection

_____
_____
_____
_____
_____
_____
_____
_____
_____
_____
_____
_____
_____
_____
_____
_____
_____
_____
_____
_____
_____
_____
_____

11. Write a letter to your past self.

Even though we may think we can accurately recollect our younger self, we recall who we were based on our current perception. While our perception has some flaws, we can still reflect on our past and think about who we were and what mattered to us. So let's revisit our perceived past self and think about who we were, how we evolved, and how things changed.

If you could go back in time and tell your past self anything, what would you say? Would you offer advice, encouragement, or tips on moving forward?

Write a letter to the person you were five, ten, fifteen, or twenty years ago. Tell your past self who you are today and the lessons you learned along the way. Give your past self pointers on how to live your best life and be the person you became. Tell your past self a story about how your past experiences led you to be exactly where you are today.

Reflection

_____
_____
_____
_____
_____
_____
_____
_____
_____
_____
_____
_____
_____
_____
_____
_____
_____
_____
_____
_____
_____
_____

12. Use a funny word.

Have you ever listened to a child make up a word and crack up at how funny it sounds? Kids enjoy playing with language and making sounds that are different and entertaining to the ear. They also love coming up with made-up words as "secrets" among friends and creating "passwords" and code-words for different situations.

Revisit that mentality. Find a word that is silly, makes you giggle, or just sounds funny. Learn its meaning and use it as much as possible. Use it in a sentence when you are chatting with someone and ACT completely normal about it. When someone looks at you with a smirk or appears confused, use it as a chance to teach the meaning of the word and why you chose to use it.

Reflection

_____
_____
_____
_____
_____
_____
_____
_____
_____
_____
_____
_____
_____
_____
_____
_____
_____
_____
_____
_____
_____
_____
_____
_____

13. Play a game.

The simple *ACT* of gameplay can get lost in the shuffle of our crazy lives and not take time to slow down. But playing games—outdoor games, board games, or card games—can bring back emotions of nostalgia and simplicity.

Think about it…what is your favorite game? Is it a sport, a board game, a card game, a pen and paper game, or even a "riding in the car" game? Whatever game you enjoy, set aside time to make sure you play it. Play the game with friends, family, or even play by yourself if it's possible. Use the game as a way to unwind, relax, and do something that you know can bring joy.

Reflection

_____
_____
_____
_____
_____
_____
_____
_____
_____
_____
_____
_____
_____
_____
_____
_____
_____
_____
_____
_____
_____
_____

14. Laugh with someone.

As we already know, laughter is the best medicine. It can alter your mood in moments. It can turn that frown upside down. And it can help fade the troubles into the background and provide relief from current concerns—even if it's only for a short amount of time.

Find someone who can laugh with you. Join them for a walk or meal, give them a ring to chat, or do whatever it takes to spend some time together sharing jokes, stories, or anything you can do that would turn into laughs. Make your goal to be laughing until your face hurts or hitting that big belly laugh that gives you a side stitch.

Reflection

_____
_____
_____
_____
_____
_____
_____
_____
_____
_____
_____
_____
_____
_____
_____
_____
_____
_____
_____
_____
_____
_____

15. Plan an event or party.

Looking forward to something exciting is often a way of getting through our daily tasks that are not always the most exciting things to do. When we have an event planned for the future, we give ourselves something to look forward to.

Maybe you already have something fun on the horizon. If so, get involved and help plan the event and organize the details to keep you excited and motivated. If you don't have any events or party planning on your agenda, start planning an event or party now for any reason that sounds exciting.

Note: The event or party does not have to be big or extravagant. It can simply be a small event, gathering, or party to celebrate something real or made up—whichever you choose.

Reflection

_____
_____
_____
_____
_____
_____
_____
_____
_____
_____
_____
_____
_____
_____
_____
_____
_____
_____
_____
_____
_____

SWEAT

— — — — — — — — — —

Good things come to those who sweat…

Sweat ACTS

Ponder this…

Do you work out?

Why or why not?

How does/would working out make you feel?

When it comes to the physical aspect of fitness, there is nothing like moving your body, working your muscles, and feeling strong. A great workout is proven to elevate your mood, release hormones, and help boost your immune system.

Sweat ACTS will make you move. They will make you use your muscles, exercise your heart, and get your blood pumping. Some *sweat ACTS* will be less about physical fitness or movement, but they will definitely challenge you and maybe even make you actually "sweat," even if they don't include a workout per se...

What will increasing your physical activity do for you?

What is a "sweat" goal you can make for yourself?

How does a daily "sweat" impact your life?

Complete these fifteen sweat *ACTS* and start feeling physically and mentally stronger.

Please be sure to consult a physician before beginning any exercise regimen and complete exercises under proper supervision.

1. Complete a race.

The feeling of accomplishment that comes with crossing a finishing line or reaching a goal is enough to create an addiction (a positive one!). However, if you don't set those goals or ever try to compete, even if only against yourself, you will never get a chance to experience that feeling.

Sign up for a virtual run, a 5K walk, or a 13.1 mile half-marathon—or go for 26.2 miles and aim to complete a full marathon! Either way, pick a race that is a little out of your comfort zone but not completely unattainable. Commit to completing it by signing up and then, work as hard as you can to make sure you cross the finish line. And remember, it isn't just about the finish line—it is about the journey to get there.

Pro Tip: Grab a friend or accountability buddy who can join you on the journey.)

Reflection

_____
_____
_____
_____
_____
_____
_____
_____
_____
_____
_____
_____
_____
_____
_____
_____
_____
_____
_____
_____
_____
_____
_____

2. Try a new workout.

New to working out? Been working out for a while? It's good for your body and mind to switch up your workout and change how you get your sweat on. Muscle confusion and pushing your body in new ways (or any way for the first time) will change your body's response, and you will reap some pretty cool physical and mental benefits.

Consider trying a workout you always considered or thought looked like fun but haven't gotten around to giving it a shot yet. Consider going to a new gym or studio, checking out online workouts to do in the comfort of your home, or joining a friend for their workout of choice. No matter how you do it, give a new workout a try.

Pro Tip: Check out our FYB Fitness platform with a variety of no equipment workouts suitable for all levels.

Reflection

_____
_____
_____
_____
_____
_____
_____
_____
_____
_____
_____
_____
_____
_____
_____
_____
_____
_____
_____
_____
_____
_____
_____

3. Commit to a goal.

What is something you truly want to accomplish that could lead to great benefits for your body and/or mind once you achieve it? Maybe it is a simple goal, such as getting more sleep. To accomplish that goal, you may have to plan to go to bed one hour earlier than usual every night this week, which will likely take some planning to accomplish.

Or maybe your goal is more involved—something like writing a book that will require work and dedication but will pay off in the end. In that case, get yourself some materials and start your outline and learn the steps it will take to bring that vision to fruition. Regardless of the end goal, set one, commit to it, and create a mini-plan with check-ins and milestones to help you reach that goal in a set amount of time. (Check the resources for our FYB goal-setting guide.)

Reflection

_____
_____
_____
_____
_____
_____
_____
_____
_____
_____
_____
_____
_____
_____
_____
_____
_____
_____
_____
_____
_____
_____
_____
_____

4. Push your limit.

We tend to stay in a space that feels comfortable, and we hesitate to push to our limits for fear of the unknown or pushing beyond and hitting a breaking point. However, without attempting to push beyond, we rob ourselves of the opportunity to find and identify our limits.

So within reason and with safety in mind, do something that will push you beyond what you perceive to be your limits. This can be a physical or mental challenge, but be prepared to feel uncomfortable and experience the natural inclination to pull back. But know that you must travel uncharted territory and get to a place you've never been to find your limits—and what you seek may even lead to surprises.

Reflection

_____
_____
_____
_____
_____
_____
_____
_____
_____
_____
_____
_____
_____
_____
_____
_____
_____
_____
_____
_____
_____
_____
_____

5. Learn a new skill.

When was the last time you learned how to do something (anything!) new? What is something you have wanted to learn to do for a while? Unless prompted, we don't often take the time to challenge ourselves to learn something new. Instead, we make excuses or find other actions or work to prioritize over expanding our knowledge or skills.

Make learning a new skill a priority. Think about what you want to learn—either from a knowledge or skill perspective—and set a goal to figure out how to make it happen. Note that this can include a physical challenge (e.g., learn to roller skate, ice skate, or ride a skateboard) or something less physically focused (e.g., learn to knit, sew, draw, etc.). Obtaining knowledge and learning new skills help us discover parts of our unknown selves and bring them to light so we can keep growing and moving toward self-actualization and fulfilling our potential.

Reflection

_____
_____
_____
_____
_____
_____
_____
_____
_____
_____
_____
_____
_____
_____
_____
_____
_____
_____
_____
_____
_____
_____
_____

6. Take a walk.

Science shows that moving your body will also move your mind. There are also proven effects of being in the great outdoors and interacting with Mother Nature that can have mood-elevating and brain-stimulating effects that help us boost productivity and bring peace and calmness.

Make time in your day to take a walk. Stand up, move your legs, and get your blood flowing and heart pumping. Walk on a path, on a trail, or around the neighborhood or through a park. Be sure to leave your phone behind and take in the sights, scenes, and smells while you stroll. And if you can't get outdoors, use a treadmill or even just walk around the office. You can use visualization and/or sounds to create your own walking "environment."

Reflection

_____
_____
_____
_____
_____
_____
_____
_____
_____
_____
_____
_____
_____
_____
_____
_____
_____
_____
_____
_____
_____
_____
_____

7. Complete a mile.

One mile is equivalent to 5,280 feet. It can take an elite athlete less than five minutes to run or an individual at an average fitness level and a casual pace around twelve minutes to walk. But no matter how you get there or how long it takes, it's still 5,280 feet.

Whether you walk, ride, swim, or run, log a full 5,280 feet and finish a mile of activity. During your mile, take time to reflect on how your body moves and feels. Shift your focus away from the physical and into the mental and get lost in your thoughts. Try to avoid looking at time or pace and just enjoy the journey.

Reflection

_____

_____

_____

_____

_____

_____

_____

_____

_____

_____

_____

_____

_____

_____

_____

_____

_____

_____

_____

_____

_____

8. Unplug your workout.

Using music or another type of media during a workout can be a great way to offer motivation or provide a distraction. We can get lost in the music and tap into our flow by zoning out and listening to an audiobook or mindlessly watching a TV show. However, sometimes, a workout without tech allows us to dip inside our own minds and either sort through some chaos or revel in the calm.

During your next workout—a bike ride, walk, run, or whatever you choose to do—give your workout a new perspective by ditching the tunes or TV and tap into a mindful practice of noticing your thoughts and what is around you. Take time to feel the sun, feel the ground under your feet, breathe in the air, hear the sounds, and see the movement around you. Be fully present in the moments of your workout and experience it from a new perspective.

Reflection

_____

_____

_____

_____

_____

_____

_____

_____

_____

_____

_____

_____

_____

_____

_____

_____

_____

_____

_____

_____

_____

_____

_____

9. Break a sweat.

Sweat is your body's natural reaction to regulate your body temperature. Meaning that when your heart starts pumping and blood starts flowing, your body reacts, and you release sweat meant to cool you down. But for those who workout, sweat is often that feel-good indicator that lets you know you are working all the parts of your body and doing something that feels good and is good for you.

Go get sweaty. Get really sweaty and hot and feel good about your body and all the things it can do. It doesn't matter how you break that sweat, but when you get there, let the sweat drip and don't apologize or even feel bad about it.

Reflection

_____
_____
_____
_____
_____
_____
_____
_____
_____
_____
_____
_____
_____
_____
_____
_____
_____
_____
_____
_____
_____
_____

10. Get physical for thirty mins.

Health guidelines often indicate that 30 minutes of exercise on a daily basis is good for your heart, mind, and waistline. The benefits of a thirty-minute sweat and endorphin-releasing session create a cycle of healthier living. And keeping a regular schedule is where the benefits truly stack up. So if you aren't into a routine yet, you can get started with one thirty-minute session. Or if you are already into working out, make sure you log thirty minutes of a physical activity that's a little different from your normal regimen.

So no matter what you do—walk, run, jump, dance—move around for at least thirty minutes. Let your heart, muscles, mind, and emotions benefit from the flow. Work toward making (at least) thirty minutes of movement a daily habit.

Reflection

_____
_____
_____
_____
_____
_____
_____
_____
_____
_____
_____
_____
_____
_____
_____
_____
_____
_____
_____
_____
_____
_____

11. Stretch your body.

One of the most important and overlooked parts of working out is recovery. Recovery includes stretching and letting your muscles rest, rebuild, and absorb all the benefits of your workout. It is also a way to ensure you maintain flexibility (which starts to deplete as we get older).

Take a few minutes in the morning when you wake up, in the evening before bed, or after a workout, and get your stretch on. Ensure you make it to at least five minutes of bending and reaching, and if it feels good, increase your time commitment. Tap into your mind and observe how you feel during each of your stretches and exhale to let the tension out of your muscles and your mind.

Reflection

_____
_____
_____
_____
_____
_____
_____
_____
_____
_____
_____
_____
_____
_____
_____
_____
_____
_____
_____
_____
_____
_____

12. Find your resting and target heart rate (and understand what it means).

While most of us understand that our heart rate increases during our workouts, we often don't understand how the heart works or why it matters.

Remember, your heart is a muscle, and it needs exercise. But it also needs to be understood. Find your resting and target heart rate numbers so you can understand how hard you should work during your workouts and how healthy your heart is at rest. Keep an eye on how your heart feels and what your heart is telling you.

Pro Tip: Use the resources section to calculate your resting, max, and target heart rate.

Reflection

_____
_____
_____
_____
_____
_____
_____
_____
_____
_____
_____
_____
_____
_____
_____
_____
_____
_____
_____
_____
_____
_____

13. Take ten thousand steps.

On average, we should aim to take about ten thousand steps every day. By taking that many steps, we set ourselves up to get some physical activity and avoid sitting too long and taking on a more sedentary lifestyle.

A great way to track those steps is to wear a pedometer or another tacker (such as a fitness watch). For a day, track your steps and see where you are in terms of a baseline. Then, gradually add steps into your day (maybe one hundred or so) to keep increasing your activity until you hit your milestone. Work your way toward that ten thousand-step goal. Once you get there, acknowledge how you did it and how it felt. Aim to continue hitting that ten thousand mark daily and keep yourself moving.

Reflection

_____
_____
_____
_____
_____
_____
_____
_____
_____
_____
_____
_____
_____
_____
_____
_____
_____
_____
_____
_____
_____
_____
_____

14. Do a push-up (or ten).

Push-ups are a great way to use a combination of essential muscles that keep you healthy and strong. However, push-ups aren't an easy exercise. Before you attempt a push-up, check out our guide (found at fuelingyourbest.com) on how to execute a proper push-up to avoid any injuries.

Work toward completing a single push-up with excellent form. After you complete your first push-up, set a goal to continue doing push-ups until you reach a magic number that you set for yourself. Push-ups aren't a magical exercise to achieve ninja status, but they do keep your upper body and core strong and give you strength that you can use daily.

Reflection

_____
_____
_____
_____
_____
_____
_____
_____
_____
_____
_____
_____
_____
_____
_____
_____
_____
_____
_____
_____
_____
_____
_____
_____

15. Learn how to squat.

A proper squat is a combination of leg and core muscles. Learning to do a proper squat can strengthen your quads and hamstrings and help keep your knees strong if you execute the squat using the correct form!

While many people watch someone squat at some point, most do so without focusing on proper form. When it comes to body movement, form is all about engaging the right muscles to strengthen your body and avoiding injury. So take the time to learn how to do a proper squat. Start squatting with proper form and work toward a consistent regimen of five to ten squats over a period of five to seven days. Quickly, you should notice an increase in muscle strength and endurance in your legs, and you may even experience a decrease in any existing knee pain.

Check out the video at fuelingyourbest.com for tips on executing a proper squat.

Reflection

_____
_____
_____
_____
_____
_____
_____
_____
_____
_____
_____
_____
_____
_____
_____
_____
_____
_____
_____
_____
_____
_____

FUEL

----- ----- ----- ----- ----- ----- ----- ----- ----- -----

FUEL your body with everything it needs so
it can provide the best place for you to live.

FUEL Acts

Ponder this…

How are you currently fueling your body?

Are you getting the fuel you need?

How do you feel and are the food choices
you're making helping or hindering your everyday
performance?

Are you taking care of your body the best you
can?

Our body is our most important tool, and it
needs to work properly. But it can only operate at its
best when we put good things into it, and we should
check in on it from time to time.

FUEL refers to what we put into our bodies to help them perform and how we take care of ourselves inside and out. FUEL *ACTS* are designed to help us become aware of how we are fueling our bodies, determine if that fuel is sufficient for our lifestyle, and ensure we check up on ourselves to make sure we are operating as we should.

What it means in terms of nutrition...

This is not about going on a "diet" but about understanding which foods have the nutrients needed to ensure your body is operating in a way that supports your lifestyle now and for the future.

Why nutrition and FUELing your lifestyle is important...

Life is about how you feel, not about how you look or measure up from a weight and inches standpoint—especially when it comes to evaluating your "health." Your self-worth is not based on your appearance or a number on the scale. But you will feel better on the inside when you are fueling your body properly, and therefore, you will look better on the outside. Keep your body in check by giving it the attention it needs from the inside out.

Complete these fifteen FUEL *ACTS* and notice how your body responds when it's properly fueled up.

1. Try a new fruit or veggie.

There are so many fruits and vegetables out there—and some that you may have never seen or heard of…which means so many opportunities to try new things to add a serving of the good stuff to your diet.

Find a fruit or vegetable that is known for its health benefits and try it for the first time—or try something you tried before but didn't like. Learn a new way to prepare it (for example, try steamed broccoli in lieu of raw broccoli) and give it a try. Acquiring the taste for a food that has health benefits will make it much easier to fuel your body the right way.

Reflection

_____
_____
_____
_____
_____
_____
_____
_____
_____
_____
_____
_____
_____
_____
_____
_____
_____
_____
_____
_____
_____

2. Make a meal that is secretly healthy.

Most of us love "good food." But our definition of good food is often based on taste and not nutrients. However, that is not to say that nutrient-rich healthy food options can't taste good. In fact, they can taste very good, and you can even find some yummy options that are healthy and can replace the not-so-healthy foods that you love eating.

Make a meal that doesn't feel like it's healthy, but it is made from all-natural, healthy ingredients. Consider making something simple such as a smoothie with spinach. Or get a little fancier and try spaghetti squash to replace traditional pasta or cauliflower rice instead of white rice. Consider it a bonus if you share it with someone else—who actually eats it—before revealing the "surprisingly healthy" ingredient list.

Reflection

_____
_____
_____
_____
_____
_____
_____
_____
_____
_____
_____
_____
_____
_____
_____
_____
_____
_____
_____
_____
_____
_____
_____
_____

3. Read food labels.

Food labels can be confusing and challenging to understand. However, the more we understand what is in our food, the better our decisions can be around what we put into our bodies. As a rule of thumb, the first ingredient on a list is generally the one with the highest amount in that food item, and if there are ingredients you can't pronounce, they are likely not-so-natural.

Go food shopping and read the food labels of your groceries before placing anything into your cart. Learn what is in your food and understand what is (and isn't) going into your body. If you see something on the ingredient list that you don't know, do a little research and learn more about it. If you don't know the majority of the listed ingredients, consider doing more research and finding a more natural option.

Reflection

_____

_____

_____

_____

_____

_____

_____

_____

_____

_____

_____

_____

_____

_____

_____

_____

_____

_____

_____

_____

_____

_____

_____

4. Know your numbers.

How much do you weigh? What is your cholesterol level? What is your blood pressure? Your resting heart rate? While all of these numbers are somewhat subjective in terms of who you are, what you do, and your physical and medical conditions, it is important to know those numbers. All of our personal "stats" provide a baseline for us to reference if we are not feeling well or experiencing any type of symptoms.

All of these numbers will help you (and your doctor) determine a "norm," and keeping a pulse on them can alert you to wave a red flag if any of the numbers make a drastic change. So get to know your numbers and use them to gauge your overall health. (But please do not let the numbers define you or make you feel bad. It's all about knowing, not beating yourself up about it.)

Reflection

_____
_____
_____
_____
_____
_____
_____
_____
_____
_____
_____
_____
_____
_____
_____
_____
_____
_____
_____
_____
_____
_____
_____
_____

5. Eat (and drink) mindfully.

When you eat, do you take the time to truly taste the food as it enters your mouth? Do you take a moment to savor the flavors and let the texture and taste simmer? And do you know when and why you are eating? Are you truly hungry, or are you bored?

We all have an eating style based on our habits, environments, and how we have consumed food throughout the years. Our eating style can help or hinder our ability to consume healthy foods in a healthy way. Being more mindful of our style can help us continue or travel down a healthy eating path and create a positive relationship with food. So for an entire day, focus on mindful eating. That means taking the time to pay attention to what you put in your mouth when you are eating and why/how you feel before, during, and after. Enjoy the flavors, take your time chewing and swallowing, and pay attention to every bite and sip.

Reflection

_____
_____
_____
_____
_____
_____
_____
_____
_____
_____
_____
_____
_____
_____
_____
_____
_____
_____
_____
_____
_____
_____

Fuel

6. Eliminate the (added) sugar.

Sweets and treats are yummy—and there is no reason to completely eliminate them from your diet forever (unless you have a medical condition that forces you to do so). Still, there can be value in eliminating and/or significantly decreasing your added sugar intake. Added sugars (not talking about naturally occurring sugars in fruit and other foods) can have unexpected—and sometimes unappreciated—effects on our bodies, minds, and habits overall.

Take a day, be mindful of your food, and eliminate any added sugar to your diet. To do this, you may have to go back to reading some food labels and focusing on the various ingredients in whatever you consume. As a general rule, avoid candy, baked goods, and anything that is made with artificial sweeteners. Notice how you feel throughout the day from a physical and mental perspective. If you feel better, notice an increase in energy, or don't see anything, try doing it again (either continue for another day or try it again in a few days).

166

Reflection

_____
_____
_____
_____
_____
_____
_____
_____
_____
_____
_____
_____
_____
_____
_____
_____
_____
_____
_____
_____
_____
_____
_____
_____

7. Research your food.

Do you know where that banana came from? Or what makes that bread taste sweet? We regularly consume food that we trust is coming from a healthful source and are often unaware of the origins or how the food landed on the plate in front of us. While we don't always have to know where our food originated, it is good to have some education on which foods are local, which are imported, and where our food is farmed.

Take some time and research three of your favorite foods—or three foods you eat the most frequently. Learn more about how those foods or brands are sourced, how they get to your local food store, and what they really contain that is good (and maybe not-so-good) for your body.

Reflection

_____
_____
_____
_____
_____
_____
_____
_____
_____
_____
_____
_____
_____
_____
_____
_____
_____
_____
_____
_____
_____
_____
_____
_____
_____

8. Track your consumption.

There is a stigma around food tracking, and that it will make you feel bad about what you are eating. In reality, food tracking is more about awareness. It is about creating an understanding of when, how, and what you eat so you can be more aware of your choices and how they impact you—or fuel you—for what you want to accomplish or how you want to perform. This information can offer some very helpful insight, so you can make lifestyle changes or dietary improvements that will help you perform at your best.

For one day, track your food consumption. Write everything in a journal or record it digitally using an app.

- Note the foods you eat, when you eat them, and how they contribute to your overall nutritional intake.
- Note your mood, feelings in your stomach, head, and anywhere else before, during, and after eating.

- Note your deficiencies or mood changes and attempt to draw correlations between what you put into your body and how you feel.

Pro Tip: The longer you do this, the more likely you will be to find patterns and extract insights. For an easy food tracking sheet, go to fuelingyourbest. com and download the food tracker sheet. You can use it as-is or modify it to meet your needs.

Reflection

_____
_____
_____
_____
_____
_____
_____
_____
_____
_____
_____
_____
_____

9. Get a physical.

When was the last time you had a physical completed by a doctor? An annual physical is meant to assess your basic health profile and offer a read on your vitals. Your visit is recorded in your medical history and becomes a baseline for medical professionals to reference year-over-year. The results are also used by other doctors and specialists if you seek medical treatment for any medical concerns.

If it's been so long that you can't remember (or honestly not within the last 365 days) since your last physical, then it's time to take care of yourself. Schedule an appointment with a primary care physician and dedicate some time to self-care and ensuring your health is a priority.

Reflection

_____
_____
_____
_____
_____
_____
_____
_____
_____
_____
_____
_____
_____
_____
_____
_____
_____
_____
_____
_____
_____
_____
_____
_____

10. Schedule a doctor's appointment.

Do you need to check the box on an annual appointment? Or has something been bothering you that you keep putting off? In general, 20 percent of adults miss an annual appointment with a doctor or specialist. This leads to missed medical conditions and overlooked issues that may become more complicated as time passes. A focus on preventative health is more effective than reacting to a found medical issue.

Take time right now to book an appointment with a doctor or specialist. Go to your yearly appointment, get a skin check, or visit a specialist that you think you should go see. And of course, make sure you keep your "health date" commitment to yourself and show up for the appointment.

Reflection

_____

_____

_____

_____

_____

_____

_____

_____

_____

_____

_____

_____

_____

_____

_____

_____

_____

_____

_____

_____

_____

_____

_____

11. Talk to a nutritionist.

Do you really understand how food works? Do you remember the food groups and how they should factor into your daily diet? Do you know what *your* body needs? Food is complicated in its creation. And how your body breaks it down and uses what it needs is the study of food science. While you don't need to get your degree in nutrition, there are some basics that can help you make better food choices.

Find a reputable, credible, educated nutritionist, and have a conversation about food. Ask lots of questions so you can work food into your diet that can help you feel good and perform at your best.

Pro Tip: Some insurance plans will cover meetings with nutritionists, so check your benefits and take advantage of the offer if it exists.

Reflection

_____
_____
_____
_____
_____
_____
_____
_____
_____
_____
_____
_____
_____
_____
_____
_____
_____
_____
_____
_____
_____
_____

12. Drink eight glasses of water.

You have probably heard it a thousand times—drink more water. Water is integral to your health, and it is so good for your body. However, most people don't consume enough to replenish on a daily basis.

So for real, set a goal to drink more water. Start with one day and ensure you consume at least eight full glasses (of at least 8 ounces) of water in a twenty-four-hour period. Note how you feel before you start drinking, while you are drinking, and after you complete your daily intake. Take notice of how you consumed the water and what a full glass feels like. Then, challenge yourself to do it again for another day. Once you see how water can be more actively consumed, it can become another healthy habit to add to your list.

Reflection

_____
_____
_____
_____
_____
_____
_____
_____
_____
_____
_____
_____
_____
_____
_____
_____
_____
_____
_____
_____
_____
_____

13. Make a smoothie.

Have you ever had a smoothie? Ever make a smoothie? Since smoothies are a great way to hide vegetables (think spinach, that when blended into a smoothie is almost undetectable by your tastebuds). Smoothies can be a great way to ensure you are filling your body full of all the good things, even if you don't have time to eat full cups of fruits and veggies.

Do some research and find a smoothie recipe that includes nutrients and healthy foods that you want to eat (or contains the nutrients you need). Make your smoothie and give it a try. Once you master your fruit to liquid to ice ratios, get creative and start adding other healthy ingredients that you might not otherwise consume.

Reflection

_____
_____
_____
_____
_____
_____
_____
_____
_____
_____
_____
_____
_____
_____
_____
_____
_____
_____
_____
_____
_____
_____
_____
_____

14. Get eight servings of vegetables.

It may sound like a lot but vegetables are so good for you, and most days, it's likely that you don't get enough. Take small steps to incorporate those healthy servings into your daily diet.

Eat carrots as a snack, put spinach in a smoothie, or hide brussels sprouts next to bacon. Whatever you have to do to make it happen, commit to getting a full eight servings of vegetables in a single day. Note how easy or challenging it was to add these foods to your diet. If it's easy, keep doing it. If you felt it was challenging, find creative recipes or different ways to prepare veggies to make them easier to eat.

Reflection

_____
_____
_____
_____
_____
_____
_____
_____
_____
_____
_____
_____
_____
_____
_____
_____
_____
_____
_____
_____
_____
_____

15. Find three healthy snacks.

When you are in a rush, what is your go-to snack? When you get the urge to crunch, what do you grab?

Revisit your food journal (if you created one) and analyze your snack cravings. Take note of the type of foods you like (for example, crunchy, salty, sweet, etc.) and identify at least three healthy substitutions that you could reach for the next time you need a quick bite. These small changes will help you make healthier decisions with ease as opposed to reaching for the next closest snack that may not be the best choice.

Reflection

_____
_____
_____
_____
_____
_____
_____
_____
_____
_____
_____
_____
_____
_____
_____
_____
_____
_____
_____
_____
_____
_____

REFLECTION

Do the work. Then, take a step back to reflect on the work you put in.

Reflections require time to consider your emotions—how you feel now, how you felt in the moment, what you loved, what you didn't—and really just understand what happened, what didn't happen, and how various *ACTS* affected you one way or another.

By evaluating your progress on a weekly basis, you take away the pressure of logging it daily, and you give your thoughts and reactions some time to marinate.

Complete a reflection each week.

Weekly Reflections

Week of: _____

Which *ACTS* did you complete this week?

_____

_____

_____

Which did you like the most and the least? Why?

_____

_____

_____

Which *ACTS* challenged you? How so?

_____

_____

_____

Overall, how did the *ACTS* make you feel?

_____

_____

_____

Weekly Reflections

Week of: _____

Which *ACTS* did you complete this week?

_____

_____

_____

Which did you like the most and the least? Why?

_____

_____

_____

Which *ACTS* challenged you? How so?

_____

_____

_____

Overall, how did the *ACTS* make you feel?

_____

_____

_____

Weekly Reflections

Week of: _____

Which ACTS did you complete this week?

_____

_____

_____

Which did you like the most and the least? Why?

_____

_____

_____

Which *ACTS* challenged you? How so?

_____

_____

_____

Overall, how did the *ACTS* make you feel?

_____

_____

_____

Weekly Reflections

Week of: _____

Which *ACTS* did you complete this week?

_____

_____

_____

Which did you like the most and the least? Why?

_____

_____

_____

Which *ACTS* challenged you? How so?

_____

_____

_____

Overall, how did the *ACTS* make you feel?

_____

_____

_____

Weekly Reflections

Week of: _____

Which *ACTS* did you complete this week?

_____

_____

_____

Which did you like the most and the least? Why?

_____

_____

_____

Which *ACTS* challenged you? How so?

_____

_____

_____

Overall, how did the *ACTS* make you feel?

_____

_____

_____

Weekly Reflections

Week of: _____

Which *ACTS* did you complete this week?

_____

_____

_____

Which did you like the most and the least? Why?

_____

_____

_____

Which *ACTS* challenged you? How so?

_____

_____

_____

Overall, how did the *ACTS* make you feel?

_____

_____

_____

Weekly Reflections

Week of: _____

Which *ACTS* did you complete this week?

_____

_____

_____

Which did you like the most and the least? Why?

_____

_____

_____

Which *ACTS* challenged you? How so?

_____

_____

_____

Overall, how did the *ACTS* make you feel?

_____

_____

_____

Weekly Reflections

Week of: _____

Which *ACTS* did you complete this week?

_____

_____

_____

Which did you like the most and the least? Why?

_____

_____

_____

Which *ACTS* challenged you? How so?

_____

_____

_____

Overall, how did the *ACTS* make you feel?

_____

_____

_____

Weekly Reflections

Week of: _____

Which *ACTS* did you complete this week?

_____

_____

_____

Which did you like the most and the least? Why?

_____

_____

_____

Which ACTS challenged you? How so?

_____

_____

_____

Overall, how did the ACTS make you feel?

_____

_____

_____

Weekly Reflections

Week of: _____

Which *ACTS* did you complete this week?

_____

_____

_____

Which did you like the most and the least? Why?

_____

_____

_____

Which *ACTS* challenged you? How so?

_____

_____

_____

Overall, how did the *ACTS* make you feel?

_____

_____

_____

Weekly Reflections

Week of: _____

Which *ACTS* did you complete this week?

_____

_____

_____

Which did you like the most and the least? Why?

_____

_____

_____

Which *ACTS* challenged you? How so?

_____

_____

_____

Overall, how did the *ACTS* make you feel?

_____

_____

_____

Weekly Reflections

Week of: _____

Which *ACTS* did you complete this week?

_____

_____

_____

Which did you like the most and the least? Why?

_____

_____

_____

Which *ACTS* challenged you? How so?

_____

_____

_____

Overall, how did the *ACTS* make you feel?

_____

_____

_____

THE FINAL ACTS

- - - - - - - - - - - -

Ultimately, the success of this challenge is up to you.

What you get out of this challenge will be in direct proportion to what you put into it.

To make the most of what you accomplished in the past ninety days, take time for your final *ACTS*— meditation, gratitude, and reflection.

THE FINAL ACT

‑ ‑ ‑ ‑ ‑ ‑ ‑ ‑ ‑ ‑ ‑ ‑

Meditation

For your final meditation, choose a meditation practice of your choice. You may choose the practice that is most beneficial for you—mindful meditation, Zen meditation, yoga, or any other method.

Take a full thirty minutes to fully immerse yourself in your meditation: no distractions, no break from the meditation—a full thirty minutes.

At the end of the thirty minutes, free write three pages of whatever comes to mind. The freewriting rules are simple: write whatever you want, do not edit or check your grammar, keep writing, and do not stop until you reach the end of the three pages.

Reflection

_____
_____
_____
_____
_____
_____
_____
_____
_____
_____
_____
_____
_____
_____
_____
_____
_____
_____
_____
_____
_____
_____
_____
_____

THE FINAL ACT

- - - - - - - - - - -

Gratitude

The final *ACT* of gratitude focuses on thanking yourself for completing the ninety days and staying committed to a positive final outcome. Therefore, your final *ACT* of gratitude is a letter that you must write to yourself.

Address yourself in the letter. Thank yourself for the ninety-day commitment. Honor your work by detailing your favorite part about the challenge and one thing you learned about yourself and one thing you learned about others or the world around you.

Avoid any negative self-talk. For example, if you skipped a day, forgot something, and didn't give all the *ACTS* your best shot, it's okay; so leave it alone and focus on the positive.

Finish the letter by expressing your emotions of gratitude—what you are grateful for in your life, the people you appreciate, and express your gratitude for being precisely in the place you are in your personal journey.

Reflection

_____

_____

_____

_____

_____

_____

_____

_____

_____

_____

_____

_____

_____

_____

_____

_____

_____

_____

THE FINAL ACT

- - - - - - - - - - - -

Reflection

For your final reflection, take a moment and jot down a few notes to answer each of the following questions.

- How do you feel after completing all ninety *ACTS* of the challenge? Consider how you feel physically and mentally. Did you experience unexpected results? Were some things harder than others?
- How long did it take you to complete the *ACTS*?
- Which *ACT* or part of the challenge was the most fulfilling? Why?
- Which *ACT* or part of the challenge was the most challenging to accomplish? What made it challenging?

216

- What was the easiest to accomplish? Why?
- What did you get out of this challenge?
- Where will you go next? Will you complete another challenge? Will you hold onto some of the lessons learned?
- What is one actionable thing you can do today to keep what you learned alive?
- How will you check back in with yourself in thirty, sixty, and ninety days? Consider setting up a "check-in" meeting with yourself in the future or finding an accountability friend.
- What will be your reminder to go through this challenge again within the next year? Will there be a time that you want to focus inward? Or an event that will prompt you to want to be your best self?

Reflection

_____
_____
_____
_____
_____
_____
_____
_____
_____
_____
_____
_____
_____
_____
_____
_____
_____
_____
_____
_____
_____
_____
_____

FINAL NOTE

You did it! Take a moment to appreciate your hard work. I am proud of you and so happy that you invested the time and effort into pushing yourself to be your best.

Keep moving forward. Keep believing in yourself. And keep the faith that if you lead with your heart and let your mind follow, that you will reach your true potential and live your life with a legacy to leave behind.

It's time for us to stand
and cheer for the doer,
the achiever, the one who
recognizes the challenge and
does *something about it.*
—Vince Lombardi

RESOURCES

- - - - - - - - - - - -

Getting started with mindfulness

What is mindfulness?

Mindfulness is the human ability to be fully present and aware of where we are and what we are doing—and to not be overwhelmed or overly reactive or by what is happening around us.

> The goal of mindfulness is to wake yourself up to the inner workings of your mental, emotional, and physical processes. This will invite you to understand who you are, where you are, what you want, and what you are capable of accomplishing.

The benefits of becoming more mindful

Whenever you bring awareness to what you are directly experiencing via your senses or your state of mind, via your thoughts and emotions, you are mindful. There is growing research that shows that when you train your brain to be mindful, you are actually remodeling the physical structure of your brain.

Mindfulness can help:

→ Reduce stress/tension (Mindfulness-Based Stress Reduction)
→ Trigger the mind to think clearly
→ Improve the ability to focus
→ Enjoy more happiness in life
→ Increase creativity and self-awareness
→ Offer greater physical health and well-being
→ Regulate sleep patterns and support relaxation

Mindfulness helps create space between ourselves and our reactions by breaking down our conditioned responses. By tuning into ourselves—our thoughts, emotions, and physical being—we can learn what we are doing and evaluate if it is beneficial or not. Once we identify those thoughts, feelings, and behaviors, we can make positive changes to move toward a more productive state of being.

Practicing mindfulness

Mindfulness is the practice of floating outside of your own mind and observing a situation from afar. It removes immediate emotion and reaction. It invites you to be still and aware so you can experience the world through a different lens.

Know that mindfulness is available to you at every moment, and the more you practice it, the more acclimated you will be to using it when you need it.

There is no one way to practice mindfulness, and how you choose to practice should be based on your interests, goals, and lifestyle.

Mindfulness can be practiced through meditations and body scans. It can be practiced by creating mindful moments, such as taking time to pause and breathe when the phone rings (instead of rushing to answer it).

While mindfulness is something you naturally are capable of doing, it is more readily available when you take time to practice on a daily basis.

Here is how you can begin a mindfulness practice:

1. *Set aside some time.* You do not need any sort of special equipment to access your mindfulness skills—but you do need to set aside time and space.

2. *Observe the present moment.* The aim of mindfulness is not to quiet the mind or attempt to achieve a state of eternal calm. Instead, the goal is simple—to pay attention to the present moment, without judgment.

3. *Let your judgments pass.* When we notice judgments arise during our practice, we can make a mental note and then let them move along.

4. *Return to observing the present moment.* Our minds often get carried away in thought, which is why practicing mindfulness is about returning—again and again—to the present moment.

5. *Be kind to your wandering mind.* No matter what thoughts pop into your head, do not judge yourself. Practice recognizing when your mind has wandered and then gently bring it back.

Consider practicing mindfulness and then working it into your daily activities in a way that helps you refocus, reframe, or relax.

MEDITATION

— — — — — — — — — — —

What is meditation?

Meditation is the practice of using a technique—mindfulness, focus, movement—to train one's attention and awareness and obtain a state of mental clarity and emotional calmness.

What types of meditation are available?

Meditation comes in many forms, but some popular options include:

- Mindfulness meditation
- Spiritual meditation
- Focused meditation
- Movement meditation
- Mantra meditation

- Transcendental meditation

How do I know which type is best for me?

Each type of meditation offers a different way to bring your mind into a state of mental clarity and emotional calmness. Some respond better by focusing on their breath and remaining in a very still state. Others can calm their mind through gentle movements of their bodies. The best way to learn which is best for you is to explore the options and see which can offer you the best mental and physical benefits.

What is the best way to begin meditating?

The best way to begin meditating is to give it a try. Start by setting a very simple goal—quiet your mind for sixty seconds. Consider doing some research to find out how you can meditate for sixty seconds to calm your mind through cues or breathing. Or if a more guided option would be more likely to set you up for success, consider using an app that will offer callouts and a guided meditation practice.

HOW TO FIND YOUR HEART RATE

- - - - - - - - - - - -

Resting heart rate

According to the American Heart Association, your resting heart rate is the number of times your heart beats per minute when you are at rest. A good time to give this a try is when you wake up and before you eat or have anything to drink.

For most of us, between sixty and one hundred beats per minute (bpm) is normal. The rate can be affected by factors like stress, anxiety, hormones, medication, and how physically active you are. An athlete or more active person may have a resting heart rate as low as forty beats per minute.

To find your resting heart rate through the old school method, check your pulse at your wrist by placing two fingers between the bone and tendon over your radial artery (which is located on the thumb side of your wrist). When you feel your pulse, count the number of beats in fifteen seconds, then multiply this number by four to calculate your beats per minute.

Maximum and target heart rate

According to the American Heart Association, your maximum heart rate is about 220 minus your age. Target heart rate during moderate-intensity activities is about 50 to 70 percent of your maximum heart rate. During vigorous physical activity, it's about 70 to 85 percent of your maximum.

About the Author

Jen Cohen Crompton is a writer, fitpro, entrepreneur, marketer, and teacher. Throughout her life, she has been an advocate for helping others live healthier and happier lives by learning to love fitness, embrace their strengths, and work toward a healthier and more holistic definition of "fitness." As a lifelong athlete and fitness guru, Jen and her husband, Jeff, opened a fitness studio in 2015 (just six months after their son was born). They had one goal: provide a welcoming, non-judgmental, and safe space to build a community of like-minded people who wanted to be healthier and happier and have fun getting there.

Through their endeavor, they invited thousands of people into their studio to enjoy boxing fitness, cycle classes, their signature Pedal and Punch, Boxing and Beats, and Cycle and Circuit formats, and made a positive impact that transcended beyond their four walls. During the pandemic, Jen launched free virtual fitness classes and online workshops to keep her community healthy and happy while providing a sense of community and purpose.

In addition, Jen launched a Boxing and Brunch program to support young women by empowering them to be confident through fitness, financial education, and general life skills that are often overlooked within the established public-school curriculum. Jen continues to push for change and to encourage each and every person she encounters to reach their full potential.

Printed in the USA
CPSIA information can be obtained
at www.ICGtesting.com
CBHW040728220124
3583CB00074B/1948

9 781662 477301